Prayer is an Adventure

Prayer is an Adventure

Patricia St John

Christian Focus Publications

Originally published in 1994
This edition © copyright 2004 Christian Focus Publications
Search the Bible © copyright Christian Focus Publications
Text © copyright Patricia St John
Illustrations by Stewart Mingham

ISBN 1-85792-840-7

Published by Christian Focus Publications,
Geanies House, Tain, Ross-shire,
IV20 ITW, Scotland,
Great Britain.

Cover design Alister Macinnes

Printed and bound in Great Britain
by Cox and Wyman.

No one version of scripture has been used in this title. It is believed that the author, Patricia St John, used her own paraphrase.

Contents

What is Prayer?

To understand what prayer is, you need first to understand yourself. Did you know that you are made of three parts and they are all important? You are made of body, mind and spirit.

With your body you communicate more with other people. You talk to them, listen to them, touch them, see them. You play with them and work with them.

With your mind you communicate more with other things; you read books, watch TV, learn at school, listen to music, enjoy entertainments.

With your spirit you communicate with God.

In our western world we hear very little about that part of us called the spirit, and that is strange because, being the only part of us that will last forever, it is really the most important. So why do we hear so little about it?

Watch your TV advertisements. You will see hundreds for the body: food, clothes, hairstyles, medicines, sport, etc. You will also see hundreds for the mind: concerts, plays, books, educational programmes, etc. But I have never seen an advertisement for the spirit. Why not?

Because the reason for an advertisement is to make money, and the things that God gives to our spirits are all free. When we ask, he gives us forgiveness, peace, courage, the knowledge of his love and he also gives us eternal life. None of these things can be bought with money. So prayer is your spirit communicating with God. It is asking him for what he longs to give. It is thanking him and telling him about our needs and the needs of those we love.

Perhaps you are not quite sure that there is a God who listens when you pray. If so, and if you really want to know him, you can pray like this: *'Oh God, I want to know you. If you are there, please make yourself real to me, or give me some sign.'*

God does not always answer at once, but if you keep on patiently praying like that, he will answer you in his own time. If a child is lost and trying to find his way home, you may be quite sure that his father and mother are also searching for him, because they love him. So if you are searching for God, you may be sure that the God who loves you is also searching for you.

A lady I know spent a long time in hospital and when she came out she was very tired and depressed. She wanted God to help her, but she couldn't feel sure that God loved her or cared for her, so she prayed something like this: *'Oh God, I need your help so much. If you are really there and if you love me, then give me some sign.'*

Nothing happened at first, but one day her husband took her and their two children to the park. They were playing and she was alone. Suddenly she saw something that reminded her of Jesus Christ and what he had done for her. What she saw was something that she described as a 'cross of sparrows' on the ground in front of her. The sparrows were there, on the ground, in the shape of a cross. She stood watching but they did not move. The cross of Jesus Christ is a sign that God loves us so much that he was willing to die for us. My friend remembered the cross of Jesus and she started to pray, knowing that God was there and would certainly help her.

God may not answer your prayer like that because he does not often treat people alike. He never made two thumbprints or two snowflakes alike, and you are special and unlike anyone else. He has a special way and a special answer just for you.

Search the Bible 1: Look up the following Bible passages to find out about a woman who prayed to God without any sound at all and a man who prayed in a very unusual place. 1 Samuel 1; Jonah 2:1. What was the woman's name and what did she pray for? In what unusual place did the man pray?

Who Am I Talking to?

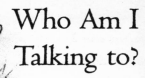

When we think about praying to God, it is good to remember how great he is. We see signs of this in his creation: the beauty of sunrises and sunsets, the never failing miracle of spring (how does that tiny seed become a flower?), the strengths of the winds and tides. When you look at a wildlife or nature programme, or listen to a talk on the mysterious universe of stars and space, or consider the marvels of your own healthy body – don't you wonder? Don't you ask who designed it all? Who thought it all out? Who keeps it all going? People nowadays will tell you that there is no Creator; that life came about from a chance fusion of atoms which evolved into higher forms. But even if I didn't believe in God, I would find that theory very difficult to accept.

I have a beautiful watch made in Switzerland and it keeps perfect time. If you said to me, 'Your watch isn't all that remarkable. Someone just threw a lot of little bits of metal into the air, and by chance they turned into your watch,' I should laugh at you. I couldn't accept that theory. But if you said to me, 'It was a clever brain and skilful hand that designed that watch,' I should believe you at once. And when I look at the power and beauty and order of the universe around me, I know that there was a Master Creator who brought it all into being. Listen to what the writers of the Bible wrote about this, thousands of years ago:

David wrote, 'When I consider your Heavens, the work of your fingers, the moon and the stars which you have set in place, what is man that you are mindful of him?'

Isaiah wrote, 'Lift up your eyes and look to the heavens. Who created all these? He who brings out the starry host one by one and calls them each by name. Because of his great power and mighty strength, not one of them is missing.'

Job wrote, 'God... spreads out the northern skies over empty space, he suspends the earth over nothing. He wraps up the water in his clouds, yet the clouds do not burst under their weight.'

I once talked to a man who said he believed in God, but he added, 'When I think of the vastness of space and the tiny dot of a planet Earth – and then I remember the relative size of one little person on earth, I cannot believe that he cares for me individually.'

But that man was wrong; later he came to realise that the Creator is also our Father. It tells us in the Bible that like a father pities his children, so the Lord pities those that fear him. It also says, 'Not a sparrow falls to the ground without the Father knowing.'

This Father wanted his children to know him, so he sent his Son to become a man – the God-Man, Jesus. And when we look at the life of Jesus in the Gospels we learn what God is like.

Jesus loved and cared about people who nobody else cared about. He touched and healed lepers who nobody else would touch. He was so patient and gentle with people whose lives were evil and sinful, that many of them finished up by becoming quite different. He had time for the children who the others wanted to send away. He comforted the sad and healed the sick and, although he was really God, he chose to live as a poor man so that he could reach and help the poor. 'This is what God is like', he said. 'If you've seen me you have seen my Father, God.'

I have heard of a huge cathedral in France with a beautiful carved ceiling. Tourists stand cricking their necks gazing upwards, but they can only see a very little at a time and get no impression of the whole.

But just as they are leaving an old man beckons to them and leads them to the font. For a few coins he removes the lid and there, mirrored in the circle of clean water, you can see a great area of the ceiling, small but perfect.

Just as that man helped others to see the ceiling, Jesus shows us what God is like because he is God. He is God's Son. We cannot look up into the sky and see the great Creator, but we can look at the perfect, spotless life of Jesus and say, 'That is what God is like'.

Search the Bible 2: In 1 Peter 3:12 we learn that God listens to prayer. Though God the Father doesn't have a body and is a spirit Peter mentions three parts of the body. What are they?

Why Pray?

There are two reasons why we should pray: God's reason and our reason. God's reason is this: He loves you and longs to communicate with you.

What a strange, sad home it would be if you came in from school, ate your tea, did your homework and went to bed without speaking a single word to your parents or taking the slightest notice of them.

How sad they would feel! They love you, and your Mum had probably been waiting for you to come and had cooked your favourite tea for you. How disappointed she would be if you just went off without so much as saying 'Hi' or 'Thanks' or 'Goodnight'.

Yet many people treat God like that. He is the great Giver. Sunshine and rain, health and the power to enjoy, light and beauty all come from him. The clothes you wore all come from him. And the food you ate today that grew in a garden or was bought in a shop all came directly from God. Yet many people never say thank you. In fact, they never think about him at all.

He is always there, looking after you and caring for you, even though you can't see him. He loves you, and love like that longs to communicate and to be loved back. Our love and our thanks are precious to him and that is the first reason why we should pray.

The second reason is that we need God's help and he gives it to those who ask for it.

Perhaps you think that you can go it alone; or if you were in real trouble, your parents would help you. But there comes times in life when we can't cope and our parents can't help us either — times of sudden disaster or illness, death or failure, the breakup of a friendship or even a home. At these times many people who never normally bother about God suddenly begin to pray.

If you never spoke to your father unless you wanted something he might quite reasonably say, 'Why should I help you? You never bother about me.'

God might quite reasonably say that, but he never does. He says, 'Call upon me in the day of trouble and I will save you.' He loves us so much that he welcomes us however and whenever we come, but he longs to give us much more than we ask for.

I heard of a man called Harry whose submarine sank to the bottom of the sea, and the crew gave themselves up for lost. But years before, in Sunday School, Harry had learned about God, and he remembered and he prayed. Wonderfully, the submarine was brought to the surface and the crew were saved. Harry did not forget. He started to read his Bible and to learn about the One who had rescued him. Now he spends his life telling people about his wonderful Saviour.

In the Bible we read of ten lepers who came to Jesus and asked to be healed. Jesus healed them all through the power of God that was in him, and they all rushed home shouting for joy. But one stopped, turned round and came back. Kneeling down, he poured out his thanks and Jesus was so glad.

'I healed ten,' he said, 'but only this one came back to thank me... Rise and go your way; your faith has made you whole.'

That leper got far more than the others; the nine rejoiced because they were made well, but the tenth got to know the Healer. He went away knowing that Jesus would always stay with him, always be his friend, always be there when he needed him.

There is another beautiful story in the Bible, in the book of Genesis, about a woman named Hagar who was journeying through the desert with her thirteen-year-old-son. They were travelling home to Egypt, and she carried food and a big pitcher of water, enough to last until the next oasis. But somehow they got lost and wandered round in circles, getting thirstier and thirstier.

And now the pitcher was empty and she looked down at her boy. His lips were cracked and his eyes glazed. He was on the point of collapse. 'We shall both die,' she thought, 'but I can't sit and watch him crying out for water.' She laid him in the shade of a desert bush and went a little distance away. Kneeling on the sand she wept and wept.

But the boy under the bush (his name was Ishmael) remembered. He had learned about God from his father and now, at the point of death, he whispered, 'Water, Lord; I need water.'

It was his mother who heard the voice: 'Hagar, look up. God has heard your boy's prayer. Open up your eyes!'

She looked up to see who was speaking but there was no one there. But right in front of her clear water was bubbling through the sand. Eagerly she filled the pitcher and ran to Ishmael. It was not too late. They drank together and went on to find the path.

So we pray for two reasons:

Firstly because God loves us and longs for us to come to him. Secondly, because we need God's help through life.

Search the Bible 3: Think about how we need God's help through life. The Psalmist David led a very dangerous life. In the poetry and songs that he wrote he talks about how powerful God is. Read Psalm 34: 17-20. What physical harm does God protect the righteous from in these verses. In Psalm 91: 5-6 what other things does God deliver his people from?

Beginning to Pray

When you start to pray, just like any other subject, it can seem very easy. As you learn more about it, it can seem more difficult but also much more rewarding. We have a snooker table in our garage, and the boys living round us come in to play. One day we were talking and I asked them if they prayed. One said, 'I prayed when my mother was ill.' Others said they never prayed. They would not know what to say.

I told them that some of the prayers in the Bible that Jesus answered were only three or four words long: 'Lord, help me,' 'Lord, save me,' 'Lord... you can make me clean.' I told them to try them out when things seemed difficult.

A few days later I went out in the car. It was pouring with rain and very cold. As I turned into the road I could see four figures huddled in the porch. As I drew up they all ran towards me.

'It works!' they shouted excitedly.

'What works?' I asked.

'What you said. We wanted to come in and we were getting so wet and cold. Then Darren said, "Lord save us." And you came round the corner.'

God hears our prayers for help and he loves to answer. Sometimes he takes away the problem; sometimes he makes us stronger and brave so that we can overcome the difficulty. John came every week for a Bible lesson and we usually prayed together. 'Is there anything special to pray about today?' I asked him.

'Yes; I've got a swimming test this week. I'm no good at swimming and I think I shall fail.'

We prayed about it and the next week I asked him how he had got on. His face brightened. 'I said to myself, "In the Name of the Lord," then I dived in and came up the other end.'

God did not take away the test. He gave him the courage and ability to pass it.

Then there is a lovely story in the Bible about a woman who did not say anything at all. She was very ill and she knew that Jesus could heal her; but when he came down the street with so many people all round him, she felt too shy to call out. But she was determined to reach him, so she started to push her way through the crowd. Weak and breathless though she was, she managed to get near enough to touch his clothes and knew at once that she was healed.

In spite of all the pushing and shoving of the crowd, Jesus felt that touch. He knew all about that woman even though she hadn't said a word. He turned round and called her, and the frightened woman knelt at his feet and told him all about it. 'Daughter', said Jesus very lovingly, 'your faith has healed you. Go in peace.'

When a baby cries out in the dark, its mother doesn't say, 'Now come along; tell me what is the matter!' She picks it up in her arms and does what needs to be done. She knows all about it without any words. And there may be times when you can't put your thoughts or feelings into words; when you just feel bored or unhappy or lonely and you can't explain why. Just remember at these times that God is there. Draw near to him in your heart, and whisper the Name of Jesus. He knows what is the matter without any words and he will comfort and help you.

But asking for help is only the beginning of prayer. It is like a beggar child coming to the door of a palace and asking for 10 pence. Supposing the King came to the door and said, 'I'll give you 10 pence but I'd like to give you much more. I'd like you to come in and be my child. Then you can ask me for anything you want. It will all be yours because you are mine.'

And this is where all real prayer begins. Although God loved us and longed to help us, we could not come close to our Heavenly Father because we were sinful and God is pure and holy. So God sent his Son, Jesus, in order to live amongst us and teach us how God wanted us to live and, in the end, to die for us.

When Jesus died, God himself was suffering and bearing the punishment for all the wrong things we had done, so that, instead of punishing us, he could forgive us and receive us as his children. So the first most important prayer we need to pray is something like this:

'Lord, I know that you love me and want me to be your child, but I know too that I have often done wrong things. Thank you for sending Jesus to die for those wrong things.

If Jesus took my punishment then I know that you will forgive me and make me your child. Now I can truly call you my Heavenly Father and come to you with all my needs and know that I am yours forever. Thank you, Father, Amen.'

When you pray that prayer write down the date because it's like a second birthday. You have been born into God's family; you are his child; now you can start talking to your Heavenly Father about everything.

Search the Bible 4: When you are asking for help it can mean that you are in a tricky situation and need a quick answer. Look up the following scripture: Nehemiah 2: 1-6. Look at how quickly God answered Nehemiah's prayer. How much time did Nehemiah spend praying in that chapter? Was it long or not?

How to Pray?

When Jesus was on earth, his disciples came to him one day and said, 'Lord, teach us to pray.' Jesus answered, 'When you pray, pray like this.' And he gave us what is called the Lord's Prayer, which you may have learned in school or in church.

Our Father who art in heaven, hallowed be your Name. Your kingdom come; your will be done on earth as it is in Heaven. Give us this day our daily bread, and forgive us our sins as we forgive those who have sinned against us. Lead us not into temptation but deliver us from evil. For yours is the kingdom, the power and the glory for ever and ever, Amen.

Jesus does not want us to recite it like parrots. He wants us to think what it means and to use it as a pattern for

27

prayer. It starts by remembering how great God is. This is called worship.

It asks that his will may be done, and that means that we shall obey him in everything.

It asks for daily bread. That means asking for what we and others need.

It asks for forgiveness; so if we know that we have done something wrong we should tell him we are sorry and ask him to help us not to do it again. We should also forgive anyone who has wronged us.

It asks for protection from evil and danger, for ourselves and for those we love.

It finishes by praising God for his greatness and goodness and for the special things he has done for us.

It is good to think about the meaning of the Lord's Prayer, but if all this seems rather long at first, remember the three first words that mothers teach their little children:

THANK YOU. SORRY. PLEASE.

THANK YOU.

Remember all the good things God has given you, all his love and all the ways he has helped you.

SORRY.

Tell him about all the things that you've done wrong. Ask him to forgive and to help you to overcome them.

PLEASE.

Ask for what you and your family and your friends need. Remember the needs of your school, your church and the world beyond. Remember that your Heavenly Father owns the universe and that you can never ask too much.

But prayer is communication, and communication means two-way talking. When you talk to your Father or to your best friend you both talk and you both listen. The Bible is full of stories of people who spoke to God and God spoke to them. We read of a king called Hezekiah. He was a good king who loved God and ruled his people well. But one day he received a terrible, frightening letter.

It was from a king in a neighbouring country saying that he was about to invade, and it was no use Hezekiah trying to resist, because his army was much, much bigger than Hezekiah's: Hezekiah might as well surrender at once.

At first Hezekiah was terrified. Then he did a very sensible thing. He took the letter to the temple (like our church) and spread it out before God. 'Lord,' he prayed, 'you read this letter and tell me what to do.'

God answered at once. He sent a message by one of his servants, a man called Isaiah. And the message was this. 'Do nothing; that heathen king will never enter this city or even shoot an arrow against it.' And that is exactly what happened. God's angel entered that great army and slaughtered so many of them that the rest turned and went home. Hezekiah prayed and God spoke to him in reply.

When we pray, we talk to God and God talks to us in different ways. Sometimes he seems to just tell us things in our hearts. Sometimes he sends messages through other people; in countries where many people can't read he sometimes speaks through dreams. But the most usual way that God speaks to us is through the Bible.

The heart of the whole Bible is the story of Jesus in the gospels (Matthew, Mark, Luke, John). So start by reading the gospels and learn from Jesus how God wants you to live. Remember that the Bible is God's voice speaking to you, so before you read it, you might pray David's prayer: 'Oh, Lord, open my eyes that I may behold wonderful things out of your Word.'

So when you want to spend time with God, make it a two-way conversation. Let God teach you from the Bible, and then pray about what you have read, as well as praying about your own special matters. It may help you to have a book that tells you where and how much to read each day, and which explains it.

Search the Bible 5: Look up the following passages to find out about three people who prayed to God. Thank you: Exodus 15:1-2. Sorry: Psalm 51: 1-2. Please: John 17.

When to Pray

The Bible tells us to pray without ceasing, but that does not mean that you are never to stop praying. If you did you would never get your lessons done or play a game. It means: always remember that God is there and you can turn to him at any moment.

When I take my little nieces to the park they let go of my hands as soon as they get close to the swings and roundabouts, and they run off to play. They seem to forget all about me as they enjoy themselves. But they feel safe and happy only because they know that I am there and that if anything goes wrong, they can run straight back to me. If I should disappear, they would no longer feel safe and happy. And prayer is sometimes just like that – feeling safe simply because God is there.

I heard of a lady who went on a train journey. She got

into the carriage and there was a tiny boy sitting all alone in the far corner. He seemed much too small to be travelling alone, and she supposed that his parents would turn up in a moment or two.

But nobody got into the carriage. Only, just before the train moved off, a man came to the window, smiled and waved at the child. The little boy smiled and waved back, then settled down to look at his comics.

After a while the lady said, 'you are very small to be travelling all alone. Aren't you frightened?'

The little boy shook his head.

'Was that your Dad who saw you off at the station?' asked the lady. The little boy nodded.

'And will someone meet you at the other end and take you off the train?' asked the lady again.

'I'm to stop in this carriage till my Dad comes and fetches me off', said the boy. 'You see, my Dad drives the train.'

That boy felt perfectly safe; his Dad was there at the beginning of the journey and would be there at the end. And all the miles between, even though the child could not see him, he was guiding the train, taking his little son in the right direction. And God our Father was there at the beginning, loving you and planning for you before you were born. He will be there at the end of the journey to take you home, and all through the years between he is caring for you and guiding you in the right way and that is why we can face life happily and unafraid, able to enjoy our work and play. We cannot think about him all the time but we know that we can turn to him at any moment and share our joys and sorrows with him. For he is not only our Father. Jesus came and lived on earth to show us that our Father can also be our best Friend.

I once heard of an Indian boy who loved football. He was playing in a match and he kicked the ball and saw it fly straight between the goal posts. 'Look, Lord Jesus!' he shouted. 'Look!' That boy wanted to share his most important moments with his best Friend.

But if you have a best friend you don't just go to them at any time, or just when you want something. You need special times when you want to be alone with them, to talk and to get to know them better.

David, who wrote most of the Psalms in the Bible, said 'Evening and morning and at noon will I pray'; and Daniel went and knelt by his open window to pray, three times a day, even when he knew that it could cost him his life. It may be impossible at school or at work to pray three times a day but the best way to grow as a Christian is to have special times that you spend alone with God.

Many people find that the best time is the early morning. It is a good start to the day to find some helpful verses in the Bible and to ask God to bless you and keep you from sin in the hours ahead. You can ask for help with the things you find difficult, and pray for your friends and family. To go into the day without meeting with God is like a soldier going into battle without his protective helmet, or a sailor going to sea without his chart and compass. David had a beautiful prayer; this is how one version of the Psalms translates it:

Cause me to hear your voice of love when I awake.

For I trust in you; Teach me your way for today,

For unto you I have handed over my life.

Then surely we won't want to go to sleep at night without telling our Father and Friend about the day that has passed. We shall want to thank him for all he has given, and ask him to forgive us where we have failed. We shall also want him to bless the work we have done and the people we love.

Here are some of the prayers that David wrote.

They are found in the Book of Psalms:

DAVID'S MORNING PRAYER

Let me hear in the morning of your steadfast love,

for in you I put my trust.

Teach me the way I should go. . .

teach me to do your will.

PSALM 143:8

DAVID'S PRAYER WHEN HE
HAS DONE WRONG

Create in me a clean heart, O God, and

put a new right spirit within me.

PSALM 51:10

DAVID'S PRAYERS FOR PURITY OF HEART

Search me, O God, and know my heart.

Try me and know my thoughts,

and see if there be any wicked way in me

and lead me in the way everlasting.

PSALM 139:23-24

Let the words of my mouth

and the meditation of my heart

be acceptable in your sight,

O Lord.

PSALM 19:14

A PRAYER BEFORE READING THE BIBLE

Open my eyes that I may behold

wondrous things out of your law.

PSALM 119:18

David also wrote a beautiful little evening prayer, probably when he was hiding in the desert rocks and caves because his enemies were trying to kill him:

I will both lay me down in peace and sleep;

for thou Lord only makest me to dwell in safety.

PSALM 4:8

Search the Bible 6: In the Bible one young man, Daniel, was brought up to pray regularly. Read the following passage — Daniel 6: 10-16. How often did Daniel normally pray? What happened when the others spotted him? Had Daniel known about what might happen as a result of praying to God instead of the king?

Does God Answer Prayer?

Consider these three answers: 'Mum, can I borrow the knife? I want to cut some string.' 'No, it is very sharp and you might easily cut yourself. Use the scissors instead.'

'Dad, can I ride to school on my BMX?'

'Wait a little. The traffic is terrible on that road, and I don't think you are experienced enough yet. In three months' time, on your next birthday, you can start riding to school.'

'Mum, Lucy has asked me to go with her family to their caravan for a week. Can I go?'

'Certainly; they are such a nice family. I'm sure you'll have a lovely time.'

Did you notice that each of these requests were answered,

but they were all answered differently? One parent said 'No', one said 'Wait', and one said 'Yes'. Did you also notice that each answer was given because the parent loved the child and cared about their safety and happiness?

In the same way, God hears and answers every prayer that you pray. Sometimes he says 'No', or 'Wait', and often he says 'Yes'. In every case the answer is given because he loves you and cares about your lasting safety and happiness; and unlike earthly parents, who can sometimes make mistakes, he always knows what is really best for us.

WHEN GOD SAYS 'NO'

In America lives a young woman who has travelled all over the world. Her name is Joni Eareckson Tada, and when she was a girl she loved sport and was a strong swimmer. One day she dived into what she thought was deep water but, actually, it was only shallow and she hit her head on the bottom and broke her neck.

She was taken to hospital and gradually it dawned on her what the doctors had known from the beginning: she was paralysed and would never be able to walk or use her hands again. She would have to be in a wheelchair for the rest of her life.

Many people prayed that Joni would be healed for, after all, others have been healed when people prayed for them. Joni herself prayed day after day, 'Oh Lord, let me walk again; give me back the use of my hands.'

Joni is still in her wheelchair; the time came when she realized that God was saying 'No', and she did not grumble or rebel. She accepted it and God began to use her in a wonderful way. She learned to write and draw beautiful pictures with a pen held in her mouth. She began to write and sing happy songs about the love of God, and people said, 'If she can sing like that, paralysed and in a wheelchair her God must be a wonderful God.' They began to write to her from all over the world, especially those who were ill and disabled. 'How can you be so happy when you are helpless in a wheelchair?' They wanted to know.

Later on Joni started to travel round and speak at meetings, and hundreds came to hear her. Later still she started to speak on television and thousands listened.

Joni understands now why God, who loves her, said 'No'. He had chosen her for a very special work: to tell the world that Jesus can bring joy and purpose to the most disabled life.

When people look at her happy face and realize that she is completely helpless and always will be... why then, they begin to believe her.

WHEN GOD SAYS 'WAIT'

Most of you will have heard people talking about Romania, that country where there was such terrible oppression and corruption, and where Christians were punished and imprisoned for their faith. Yet in spite of the danger, some of them went on reading their Bibles and talking about Jesus in secret, and one of these was a woman called Ada. She used to travel about quietly gathering people together and she loved to teach children about God, their Heavenly Father.

One day Ada had been out to a distant village. The only way to get home was to hitch a lift, and she stood by the road praying silently. 'Lord, make the right car stop for me,' she whispered, but no one took any notice of her. Car after car passed her, her outstretched hand waving in vain.

It was cold and wet, and after an hour or so it began to rain hard. She began to feel very impatient. 'Really Lord,' she whispered, 'you could stop a car for me so easily... why don't you?' So she went on praying whilst her coat and feet got wetter and wetter. It began to get dark and much colder, and poor Ada was in tears. She wondered whether she would have to wait until morning.

She had been waiting for three hours and had almost given up hope when a bus came along and stopped right in front of her. This was most unusual, but she climbed on thankfully and sat down on the last bench with water dripping from all over her.

She told the conductor how far she wanted to go and bought her ticket but the sound of her voice made a little boy in the front turn round. He looked at her for a moment and then his eyes became big and his face lit up. He made his way quickly to the back and ran to Ada, putting his arms round her wet scarf.

'I've found you, I've found you at last,' he whispered. 'I've been praying so much to find you again.'

Ada looked at him in surprise.

'Don't you remember me?' the boy said softly.

'You told me about Jesus and you gave me this.' He

45

pulled out from the inside pocket of his jacket a worn-out Christian booklet. 'I received Jesus into my heart and I'm his child now. I've been praying for one year to find you again.'

Quietly they talked together and exchanged addresses, and when at last Ada got home, very tired and wet, she prayed something like this: 'Thank you, Lord! It was worth waiting in the rain to meet that child. Thank you so much for stopping the right bus for me.'

WHEN GOD SAYS 'YES'

The following story comes from those exciting early days just after Jesus had gone back to heaven, and the twelve disciples were starting on their dangerous task of telling the world that the Jesus that they had crucified was actually alive and active, although they could not see him. It all made King Herod, who had been partly responsible for Jesus' death, very anxious and angry and he ordered his soldiers to arrest anyone found teaching this truth.

But the disciples simply couldn't stop talking about it, so James was the first to go when the king ordered him to be beheaded. Peter was taken next and put in prison overnight. He was to be executed next morning.

But Herod knew that strange things had happened to the followers of Jesus and he decided to take no risks. He ordered sixteen soldiers to guard this one prisoner and two of them were to be double-chained to him all night. No possibility of anything going wrong this time, thought Herod the King!

It seems that Peter was not unduly worried; after all, just a few hours more and he would see Jesus again. He lay down between the two soldiers, arranged his chains as comfortably as possible, and went to sleep.

Suddenly he woke up for someone had shaken him; a light was shining in the cell and one of God's angels was standing there beside him. 'Quick! Get up!' said the angel, and the chains simply slid off Peter's wrists. 'Get dressed and put on your shoes,' said the angel, and Peter obeyed. All the guards were still soundly asleep.

'Follow me,' said the angel and Peter did so. He was quite sure that he was dreaming as he walked through the first and second locked prison doors and reached the great outer iron gate. It opened of its own accord and Peter felt the fresh night air on his face. He was in the street, walking down it with the angel. But after a short distance the angel disappeared and Peter was left alone in the dark.

'This is no dream,' said Peter to himself, rubbing his eyes. 'It has really happened; God has saved me from death, but I'd better move on as quickly as I can. I'll go to Mary's house, mother of my friend, John Mark. They will probably be awake, praying for me.'

What Peter did not know was that the whole group of Christians had come together that night to pray for their leader, Peter. They needed him so much. No one felt like going to sleep; they just went on praying through the night, 'Oh Lord, save Peter.'

Suddenly as they prayed there was a soft knock at the door. A girl named Rhoda went, very cautiously indeed, to see who was there.

'Who is it?' she asked quietly.

'It is I, Peter,' came the whisper form outside.

Rhoda was so excited that she forgot to open the door. She rushed back into the prayer meeting. 'You can all stop praying,' she cried, 'Peter is here, at the door.'

They all stared at her.

(Knock, knock.)

'You're crazy,' said one.

(Knock, knock.)

'Impossible!' said another.

(Knock, knock!)

'It must be his ghost,' said someone. 'That means they have killed him already.'

(Knock, knock.)

'Well, somebody's there,' said someone else. 'Hadn't we at least better have a look?'

Very cautiously indeed they crowded to the door.

'Who's there?' they whispered.

'I, Peter,' came the answer. 'Let me in quick and don't make a noise.'

Still hardly believing, they opened the door a chink and Peter slipped in, motioning them to keep very quiet. Then as they crowded round him, he told his incredible story, in a low voice. 'I daren't stay here', he said when he had finished, 'I'd better move on to somewhere safer. But tell the others that I'm free and that their prayers are answered.'

It was good that those people prayed but what a pity they did not believe that God could answer their prayers.

Don't be like that. We are told to pray in faith, believing. Watch for God's answers, expecting them to come, even if they are not the exact answers you asked for. He knows the best answer and he is always listening and always caring and loving.

So get started on life's greatest adventure: learning to pray.

Search the Bible 7: Look up Philippians 4:4-7. What does God tell us to be in those verses and what does he tell us not to be? What is the key thing that he tells us to do in these verses and what will God give you when you do this?

The Holy
Spirit Helps

A s you keep on praying, you will begin to realise
that you have an enemy in prayer and a helper
in prayer.

Satan is our enemy in prayer. He wants us to be sinful
and miserable and weak. He hates us to pray, because God
has promised that when we pray, people will be forgiven
and joyful and helped and made well and delivered from
evil. So Satan does all he can to stop us praying.

He will whisper in your heart that you are too busy,
that it does not really matter and that other things are more
important than prayer. Even when you do pray, he will make
you think about other things, so that you forget you are
meant to be praying.

But the Holy Spirit, who lives in the heart of every true

Christian, is our helper in prayer. There is a verse in the Bible that says: 'The Holy Spirit helps us... in our praying; for we don't know how to pray as we should, but the Holy Spirit prays for us' (Romans 8:26; the Living Bible).

The Holy Spirit is stronger than Satan. He can give us victory over our enemy. He knows what we mean even when we cannot put it into words. He takes our longings and cries for help and lifts them up to God, not always as we say them but as we really mean them.

When I was a child I heard a story that I have never forgotten. It was about someone who had a very strange dream.

He dreamed that a messenger led him into a church where five people were kneeling in prayer, and in front of each sat a white bird with folded wings.

'Watch these people at prayer,' he was told, 'and notice what happens to the white birds.'

So the dreamer watched the first person. She was a woman beautifully dressed, kneeling right in front of the church. She prayed with her face lifted and the words flowed from her lips. Her white bird was the largest and finest and whitest of them all, but although she prayed and prayed, it never moved at all nor fluttered a feather.

'Put out your hand and touch it.' The man did so.

In his dream he reached out and gently touched the perfect white feathers and drew back his hand hastily. 'I believe it's dead,' he said.

'Yes,' was the sad reply 'it's quite dead. The woman has been to church since childhood. She puts on her best clothes and she knows all the best prayers by heart. Her words are so beautiful, but she does not mean them, and when she leaves the church she forgets all about them. She does not even think about what she is saying. Look! She is glancing at her neighbour in the next pew and wondering how much her hat cost.'

The dreamer moved to the second kneeling figure. He seemed to be praying very nicely. The beautiful white bird in front of him stirred its feathers and soared upwards and the dreamer, following its flight, noticed that the church had no roof. Up it mounted straight into the blue.

But suddenly the face of the praying man changed. His devout expression became hard and bitter, and he pressed his lips together, and muttered something under his breath. Then the beautiful soaring bird dropped as though an arrow had pierced it and lay dead on the church floor. The dreamer was very puzzled.

'That man started to pray sincerely,' was the answer 'but as he prayed he remembered someone who had wronged him. Anger flooded into his heart and he turned from love. He will not forget and he will not forgive. See, he is hurrying out to plan some revenge.'

The dreamer paused before the third praying figure. A woman was kneeling, her hands clasped, the marks of tears on her cheeks. As she prayed the fair white bird in front of her began to rise and then sank again, summoned its strength and rose, almost reached the top of the pillar, and then seemed to fall. But before it reached the ground it struggled up again beating its wings, and at last it reached the clear blue air, fluffed out its feathers and disappeared into the sunshine.

The dreamer and his messenger drew a sigh of relief.

'This woman has passed through great sorrow and could no longer believe that God loved her or cared for her. She has not been here for a long time, but today she came back and tried to pray. But as she prayed her doubts returned ... she could not believe... she nearly gave up; but she told the

Lord about her doubts and whispered the promises of God, and her faith was strengthened. God has heard her prayer and he will comfort her!'

The fourth kneeling figure looked like a tramp from the streets, and in front of him huddled such a weak, dingy bird, which looked as though it could not rise at all. The man did not even seem to be speaking, he just looked wretched. But all of a sudden the dull wings quivered and the bird flew straight upwards in strong flight. And as it reached the open sky, its wings, kissed by the sunshine, gleamed white as snow and the messenger laughed for joy.

'That man does not know how to pray at all,' said the angel. 'He has never prayed in his life and does not know what words to use. But his heart is heavy with his sin and need, and his thoughts are crying out for mercy and forgiveness. Just at this moment all the angels of God are rejoicing because another sinner has come home.'

The last person in the church was a little boy, and in front of him sat a tiny, spotless bird. The child folded his hands and said that he was sorry that he had slapped his sister, and asked God to make his mother well and please to help him with his sums. He thanked God for the football he got on his birthday, and the bird flew straight upwards with a song of joy, and the child jumped up and ran out into the garden to kick his ball, laughing up into the face of the dreamer and the messenger as he passed by.

Search the Bible 8: In the following two Bible passages it talks about people who look as if they are praying but aren't really. It also talks about people who think they are praying in a way that pleases God but aren't really. Who were they? Who was the man who was really praying to God? Why did God exalt him in the end? Mark 12:40; Luke 18:9-14.

Prayers for You to Use

So when you pray, remember it is not what you say or how you say it that matters, but the really important things are: Is my heart right with God? Do I want the things that he wants? Do I really believe that he hears me?

That is where the Holy Spirit helps us. Listen to his voice as you pray. He reminds us of things that are wrong, so we can ask to be forgiven and put them right. He reminds us of people who need our prayers. He strengthens us and comforts us when we feel like giving up prayer altogether, and he makes us love Jesus. So get started on your great life-adventure of praying.

On the next pages are some prayers that will help you to start praying. Some are from the Bible and some have been written by young people, just like you. If you cannot think of your own words at first it does not matter. Perhaps one of these prayers will express just what you are thinking and you can use that instead.

You will see that in the Bible, just as today, people turn to God in every kind of circumstance – when they are happy and thankful, and when they are worried or sad. Because God loves us, he is interested in everything that happens to us; there is nothing that is too small or unimportant to tell God.

Some prayers only contain three or four words, and none are long. We do not impress God by using clever words, and he would rather hear a ten-second prayer that is simple and sincere than a ten-minute one that is not from the heart.

Just as our parents tell us we must not be selfish with our things, God does not want us to be selfish with our prayers. Some people cannot pray for themselves; perhaps they are too ill, or too sad or too frightened to be able to remember that God is near them. Among these prayers you will find some which ask God to protect people in countries where there is war, or famine. Another prayer asks God to look after the homeless. Another asks God to show us what *we* can do to help people in need. When you see pictures of sad events on television or in newspapers and you wonder what can be done to help, perhaps this is the Holy Spirit prompting you to ask God for this help.

Some lines from well-known hymns are also included. No one has ever said that we must always *talk* to God, we can sing to him too! And it need not stop there, as the Psalmist says:

Sing to the joy of the Lord, all the earth...

Sing praises to the Lord!

Play music on the harps!

Blow trumpets and horns,

and shout for joy to the Lord, our King.

PSALM 98:4-6

Search the Bible 9: The Bible says something about the prayer of a righteous person. Look up James 5:16 to find out what.

Some Bible Prayers

A PRAYER OF PRAISE AND THANKS

O Lord, Our Lord, your greatness is seen in all the
world! Your praise reaches to the heavens;
it is sung by children and babies.

Psalm 8:1-2

MOSES' PRAYER

I am nobody. How can I go to the king and
bring the Israelites out of Egypt?

Exodus 3:11

MOSES' PRAISE

Lord, who among the gods is like you?
Who is like you, wonderful in holiness?
Who can work miracles and mighty acts like yours?

Exodus 15:11

HANNAH'S REQUEST

Almighty Lord, look at me your servant! See my trouble
and remember me! Don't forget me! If you give me a son, I
promise to dedicate him to you for his whole life.

I Samuel 1:11

HANNAH'S PRAYER OF THANKS

The Lord has filled my heart with joy; how happy I am
because of what he does! I laugh at my enemies;
how joyful I am because God has helped me.

I Samuel 2:1

SAMUEL'S PRAYER WHEN HE HEARS
GOD CALLING

Speak; your servant is listening.

I Samuel 3:10

DAVID'S PRAYER FOR FORGIVENESS

Be merciful to me, O God, because of your constant love.
Remove my sin and I will be clean;
wash me and I will be whiter than snow.

Psalm 51:1 & 7

DAVID'S PRAYER WHEN IN DANGER

When I am afraid, I put my trust in you.
What can a mere human do to me?

Psalm 56:4

DAVID'S PRAYER AT
THE END OF HIS LIFE

Lord God, may you be praised for ever!

You are great and powerful, glorious, splendid and majestic.

Everything in heaven and earth is yours and you are king,

supreme ruler over all. All riches and wealth come from you;

you rule everything by your strength and power; and are

able to make anyone great and strong. We give you thanks,

and praise your glorious name. Yet we cannot really give you

anything, because everything is a gift from you, and we have

only given back what is Yours already.

I Chronicles 29:10-14

SOLOMON'S PRAYER FOR HELP

O Lord God, you have let me succeed my father as king, even

though I am very young and don't know how to rule. Here I

am among the people you have chosen to be your own,

a people who are so many that they cannot be counted. So give

me the wisdom I need to rule them with justice and to know

the difference between good and evil. Otherwise, how would

I ever be able to rule this great people of yours?

I Kings 3:7-9

ELIJAH'S PRAYER FOR HELP

O Lord, the God of Abraham, Isaac and Jacob, prove that
you are the God of Israel and that I am your servant and
have done all this to your command. Answer me, Lord, so
that this people will know that you, the Lord, are God and
that you are bringing them back to yourself.

I Kings 18:36-37

ISAIAH'S PRAYER OF DEDICATION

Here I am. Send me.

Isaiah 6:8

JEREMIAH'S PRAYER WHEN NERVOUS

Sovereign Lord, I don't know how to speak;
I am too young.

Jeremiah 1:6

JONAH'S PRAYER FROM INSIDE THE FISH

In my distress, Lord, I called to you and you answered me.

Jonah 2:2

MARY'S PRAYER

I am the Lord's servant,

may it happen to me as you have said.

Luke 1:38

MARY'S PRAYER OF THANKS

My heart praises the Lord; my soul is glad because of God

my Saviour, for he has remembered me, his lowly servant.

From now on all people will call me happy, because of the

great things the Mighty God has done for me.

Luke 1:46-49

JESUS TEACHES HOW TO PRAY

Our Father in heaven, hallowed be your name, your

kingdom come, your will be done on earth as it is in

heaven. Give us today our daily bread. Forgive us our

debts as we also have forgiven our debtors. And lead us

not into temptation, but deliver us from the evil one.

Matthew 6:9-13

A SICK BOY AND A PRAYER FOR HELP

I do believe; help me overcome my unbelief!

Mark 9:24

BLIND BARTIMAEUS' PRAYER

Jesus! Son of David! Take pity on me!

Mark 10:47

PETER CRIES FOR HELP

Lord, save me.

Matthew 14:30

JESUS PRAYS BEFORE HIS DEATH

Father, the hour has come. Give glory to your son, so that
the Son may give glory to you.

John 17:1

JESUS PRAYS FOR ALL WHO FOLLOW HIM

I pray that they may all be one in order that the

world may know that you sent me and that

you love them as you love me.

John 17:23

Search the Bible 10: The Bible tells us to
pray for lots of different people. Here are a
few examples — Ephesians 6:18; Luke 6:28;
Matthew 26:41.

Prayers for Special Occasions

WHEN YOU WANT TO SAY

'THANK YOU'

I will sing to you, O Lord,

because you have been good to me.

Psalm 13:6

How wonderful are your gifts to me;

how good they are!

Psalm 16:6

Patricia St John

Give me joy in my heart, keep me praising.

Jesus! my shepherd, brother, Friend,

My Prophet, Priest and King,

My Lord, my Life, my Way, my End,

Accept the praise I bring.

John Newton

For the beauty of the earth,

For the beauty of the skies,

For the love which from our birth

Over and around us lies,

Patricia St John

Lord of all, to thee we raise

This our sacrifice of praise.

F. S. Pierpoint

WHEN YOU WANT TO SAY 'SORRY'

Lord Jesus Christ, Son of God,

have mercy on me, a sinner.

Luke 18:38

Just as I am, thou wilt receive,

Wilt welcome, pardon, cleanse, relieve:

Because thy promise I believe,

O Lamb of God, I come.

Charlotte Elliot

Wash away all my evil

and make me clean from my sin!

Psalm 51:2

My sacrifice is a humble spirit, O God;

you will not reject a humble and repentant heart.

Psalm 51:17

Dear Lord and Father of mankind,

Forgive our foolish ways.

J. G. Whittier

WHEN YOU ARE SAD

The Lord hears me weeping; he listens to my cry for
help and will answer my prayer.

Psalm 6:9

I will be glad, because you will rescue me.

Psalm 13:5

The night becomes as day,

When from the heart we say,

May Jesus Christ be praised;

The powers of darkness fear,

When this sweet chant they hear,

May Jesus Christ be praised.

E. Caswall

Why am I so sad? Why am I so troubled?

I will put my hope in God and once again

I will praise him, my Saviour and my God.

Psalm 42:5

Ask and it will be given to you; seek and you will find; knock and the door will opened to you. For everyone who asks receives; he who seeks finds; and to him who knocks, the door will be opened.

Matthew 7:7-8

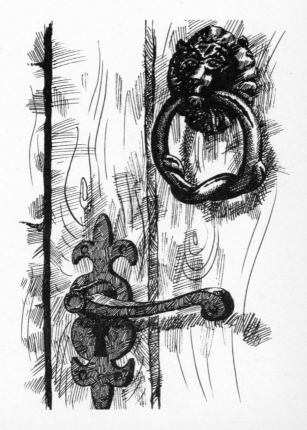

WHEN YOU ARE WORRIED OR FRIGHTENED

Father, my Father!

All things are possible for you.

Take this cup of suffering away from me.

Yet not what I want, but what you want.

Mark 14:36

When I was in trouble,

you helped me.

Be kind to me now

and hear my prayer.

Psalm 4:1

You bless those

who obey you, Lord;

your love protects them

like a shield.

Psalm 5:12

You, Lord, are all that I have and you give me all I
need; my future is in your hands.

Psalm 16:5

O God our help in ages past,

Our hope for years to come,

Be thou our guard

while troubles last

And our eternal home.

Isaac Watts

WHEN SOMEONE HAS HURT YOU

Forgive them Father!

They don't know

what they are doing.

Luke 23:34

You take notice

of trouble and suffering

and are always ready to help...

you have always helped the needy.

Psalm 10:14

The Lord protects

and defends me;

I trust in him.

Psalm 28:7

WHEN YOU FEEL ALONE

Remember me, Jesus.

Luke 23:42

When I lie down, I go to sleep
in peace; you alone, O Lord, keep
me perfectly safe.

Psalm 4:8

My father and my mother may abandon me,

but the Lord will take care of me.

Psalm 27:10

Dear Lord, help me remember your promise,
'I will always be with you; I will never abandon you.'
You are all round me on every side; you protect me
with your power... where could I go to escape from
you?... if I went up to heaven you would be there; if I
lay down in the world of the dead, you would be there.

Psalm 139:5, 7-8

WHEN YOU ARE HAPPY

Praise God, from whom all blessings flow, praise him,
all creatures here below, praise him above, angelic
host, praise Father, Son and Holy Ghost.

Thomas Ken

O Lord, our Lord, your greatness
is seen in all the world.

Psalm 8:1

I will praise you, Lord, with all my heart;
I will tell of all the wonderful things you have done.
I will sing with joy because of you.

Psalm 9:1

Your presence fills me with joy
and brings me pleasure for ever.

Psalm 16:11

PRAYERS FOR GUIDANCE

Teach me your ways, O Lord.

Psalm 25:4

Teach me, Lord, what you want me to do,

and lead me along a safe path.

Psalm 27:11

The Lord is my Shepherd...

he guides me in the right paths.

Psalm 23:1, 3

God be in my head and in my understanding;

God be in my eyes and in my looking;

God be in my mouth and in my speaking;

God be in my heart and in my thinking;

God be at my end and in my departing.

Teach me, my God and king,

In all things thee to see,

And what I do in anything

To do it as for thee.

George Herbert

FOR A BIRTHDAY OR SPECIAL DAY

This is the day that the Lord hath made,

He calls the hours his own;

Let heaven rejoice, let earth be glad,

And praise surround the throne.

Isaac Watts

You created every part of me;

you put me together in my mother's womb...

when I was growing there in secret,

you knew that I was there –

you saw me before I was born.

Psalm 139:13,15

Praise the Lord, my soul!

I will praise him as long as I live;

I will sing to God all my life.

Psalm 146:1-2

This is the day of the Lord's victory;

let us be happy, let us celebrate!

Psalm 118:24

CHRISTMAS

Let us praise the Lord...

he has provided us a mighty Saviour.

Luke 1:69

O Come let us adore him.

Frederick Oakley (1802-1880)

Thou didst leave thy throne and thy kingly crown,

When thou camest to earth for me;

But in Bethlehem's home

there was found no room

For thy holy nativity:

O come to my heart, Lord Jesus;

There is room in my heart for thee.

Emily Elliot

What can I give him, poor as I am?

If I were a shepherd, I would bring a lamb;

If I were a wise man, I would do my part;

Yet what I can I give him – give my heart.

Christina Rossetti

Sovereign Lord, my eyes have seen your salvation

which you have prepared in the sight of all people,

a light for revelation to all the world

and glory for your people Israel.

Simeon

Luke 2: 29-32

EASTER

I sometimes think about the Cross,

And shut my eyes and try and see

The cruel nails and crown of thorns,

And Jesus crucified for me.

But even could I see him die

I could but see a little part

Of that great love which, like a fire

Is always burning in his heart.

And yet I want to love thee, Lord

O light the flame within my heart

And I will love thee more and more

Until I see thee as thou art.

W. Walsham How

Where, Death, is your victory?

Where, Death is your power to hurt?

But thanks be to God

who gives us the victory

through our Lord Jesus Christ!

1 Corinthians 15:55,57

Jesus Christ is risen today, Alleluia!

Lyra Davidica

FOR MY FAMILY

Dear Lord, you know our family is going on
holiday. Please let it be a happy time and look after
my dog who is staying behind, and don't let him
miss me too much.

Joe 12

Dear God, thank you that we are going on holiday
in the caravan. Please help my Mum and her friend
to cope with all the kids who are going. Help me to
be grateful, let me have fun at the beach and
swimming pool. Bless my Mum and Gavin's Mum
for taking us.

Jeremy 12

Dear Jesus, thank you for Mum, Dad, our dog
and pets. Thank you for my friends and for taking
care of us.

Robert 8

Dear Lord Jesus, let me say thank you for a lovely
day. Thank you, too, for my big brother and my
father and my mother. Thank you, Lord for all
your care and for things that I can share. Thank

you, Lord, you're always near so there's nothing I need fear. And again, dear Lord, I say thank you for a lovely day.

Paul 13

Dear Lord Jesus, thank you that you are always with me. Thank you for my home, for my Mum and Dad, and for my food, and thank you that you love me. Amen.

Peter 7

Dear Lord, please bring Mum and Dad together at home soon, so we can be a happy family again. You know I sometimes feel afraid. Please help me to trust you more and to know you are always close beside me.

Jane 10

FOR FRIENDS AND
THE FUN WE ENJOY

Thank you, Lord, for friends. Help me to be a good
friend to other people, and to notice if there is
someone lonely; may I be able to make her feel
she's wanted too.

Kate 11

Please, Lord, help us play our best in the football
match. You know we want to win, but help us not to
mind too much if we don't.

Ted 11

Dear Father, thank you for getting us off the street
and that we can all be together to play and to talk
and to learn about you at Girl's Club. Thank you for
the helpers and that they take us out on trips.

Jenny 11

THANK-YOU PRAYERS

Dear God, thank you for your kindness and help
and the good things you give us. Thank you for
school and for friends. Help them to come to
love you too.

Sally 10

Thank you, Lord, for the Bible and what we learn
about you. Help me to live in the way you want.

Mark 13

Thank you, Lord, that you love me all the time,
even when I forget you.

Emma 10

Thank you, Jesus, for all you have done for me.
May my life somehow show that I belong to you.

Kelly 12

Thank you, Jesus, for dying for me and forgiving sin.
Peter 8

Father in heaven, thank you for being my friend. I
love you and want to worship you well. Help me to be
kind. Thank you for being my Father.

Lucy 6

Dear Father, thank you for Patricia St John and her books. Thank you for all the children round the world who are reading her stories. Thank you for all the books that I have. Please help these children to find out about how much you love them.

Anna 11

Thank you, Lord Jesus, for the happiness of Spring with the new-born animals that fill our countryside. Please bless the animals of our world and help those who are being badly treated.

Katherine 10

Dear Father, we thank you for looking after us and loving us, and the most important thing is making us love you back a lot. We can never love you as much as you love us, but we try our best. In Jesus' name.

Robert 13

FOR PEOPLE IN NEED

Thank you for my birthday and my bicycle and computer games. Help me to remember children who are starving, and show me how to help them.

Ryan 10

Lord, we want to pray for John's mother who is having an operation. Let her know that you are with her and please make her well again soon.

Andria 13

Thank you, Lord, for our homes and for our food and drink. Help the people in the countries where they haven't got enough to eat, and let there be peace where people are fighting and being killed.

Jonathan 11

Dear God, thank you for all you give us, birds, sunshine, flowers and all the things that make us happy. Please let there be peace where there is war. Help children who are made orphans. Give them somewhere to go, and someone to look after them and love them. In Jesus' name. Amen.

Sarah 13

Dear Lord Jesus, please help the children in those countries that are at war where they don't even have beds to sleep in or food to eat. Please let there be peace soon.

Gabriel 9

Dear God, I pray for all those that are homeless. Please let there be people who will think about them and be able to help them.

Barak 11

Dear Lord, thank you for our homes. Please help the children who are in places where there is war. May they soon find a home again and be able to live at peace. Show us some way that we can help.

Tom 13

FOR MY SCHOOL

Dear God, thank you for helping me to get my maths test right and for getting me a silver star. Many thanks, too, for forgiving me when I have done something wrong.

Lindsay 10

Please, Lord, help me in the test tomorrow so that I'm not told off.

David 9

Lord, I want to thank you for being good to me. Thank you for my school and for good teachers. Please help the school council to find the right person to be our teacher next year. Amen.

Karen 10

Dear Jesus, please help us at school tomorrow because we all find it hard at times to love everyone; but we know how much you love us all, whether we're good or bad. I just can't do that, so please help me, Lord, so that if I don't like someone I'll be able to see some good in her and come to like her in the end.
In Christ's name – Amen.

Rachel 12

Dear Lord, please help me to get on well at Secondary School, and to be in the same class as my friends. Help me to keep my temper under control when my brothers tease me.

Hannah 11

Please, Lord, help me not to quarrel and fight with people. Let me remember that you love them too.

David 10

Thank you, Lord, that you forgive. I want to be good but often I'm not. Help me to say sorry and do better.

John 9

Lord, you know it isn't always easy to pray. Help me to read your word and listen to you so I can know you in a real way.

Tom 12

Dear God, help me not to mind when things don't go my way. Help me to put you first and others before me. Thank you for sending Jesus to save us from sin.

Caro 10

Dear Father, please help me not to be angry with people who hit me or are mean to me. Help us to be friends. Please help me not to be scared at night. I love you and I am glad you are always with me.

James 10

Dear God, please help me in all I do and teach me to follow you. You are the only one that will be with me in everything I do. Please help others who don't know you yet to find you too, and keep us all safe in your strong arms. I love you Lord, Amen.

Jenna 8

Prayers of Belief

Thank you Father, that you love me more than any earthly father. All love flows from you. Thank you for your love that never forgets me, even when I forget you; that always welcomes me back even when I sin; that loves to forgive me even when I don't deserve it.

O God, my Father and Creator, thank you that you created me for yourself and loved me even before I was born. Thank you for coming to me in Jesus, and paying the price of sin, when Jesus died. Help me to give myself to you. Thank you for redeeming me.

God, I know you are the only one who can make me happy. My sin is a barrier between us but Jesus bore it away. Help me to understand that, if I trust him I can come to you at any moment. Thank you that you are preparing a home for us in heaven. Make me ready for when you shall call me.

Prayers of Trust

Thank you, Lord, for your care over me, all day and night – when I play and climb and swim, when I travel on the roads. Thank you for any time in my life when I have been ill or in danger and you have saved and protected me. Keep, by your love and power, any who are in danger tonight – any I know in countries at war, any who are unjustly imprisoned, any who are suffering because they are Christians. Help them to know that nothing can separate them from your love. May your love take away their fear, and may they be comforted and strengthened. Give them peace and courage today.

Lord, when I am in difficult situations and don't know how to act, give me your wisdom. When I have an opportunity to speak for you, and don't know what to say, give me your words. Keep me in close contact with yourself so I can draw on your resources at any moment, and thank you that you are always there.

Lord, I want to thank you for the things you send into my life that seem hard and disappointing. Help me to believe that they too are part of the pattern of my life. Keep me from grumbling and doubting. Keep me joyful and praising because I trust in you.

Thank you, Lord, for the joy and strength and beauty of those who have died trusting in Jesus, and thank you for the day when we shall all meet again.

Thank you, Jesus, for your promise that you will come back and take your children home. Even though I do not know when this will be, teach me to live, ready and waiting for your coming. Thank you for the wonderful happiness that we shall know when we see you. 'He who gives his testimony to all this says, 'Yes indeed! I am coming soon!' (Revelation 22:20) So be it, come, Lord Jesus.

Prayers of Love and Thanks

Lord, I understand that you loved me enough to die for me, that I might have eternal life, and you will call me to come and shelter in Jesus from sin and eternal death. Teach me to answer your call. Thank you for loving me; thank you for dying for me.

Lord Jesus, when I think about your sufferings and the wounds on your hands, help me to understand how much you loved me. Help me to hate the sin that made you suffer so, for it was I who ought to have suffered. Help me to overcome sin, and turn from it. Teach me to love you, because you loved me so much.

Thank you, Lord, that you took my sin so that you could clothe me in your righteousness. Help me day by day to to show others how clean and good and beautiful the Lord Jesus is. Teach me to understand how this can be. Teach me to love the one who died for me.

Lord, I am thankful that you went right through death and came back to tell us not to be afraid. I am glad that for those who love and trust you death is just the last part of the way home. Thank you for the joy of those who have gone ahead. Thank you that we shall see them again.

Lord Jesus, I am so glad that you came back from the dead and that you are alive today. I thank you that, if you are with me, I need never feel lonely or afraid, and that nothing can really hurt me if I walk through my life with you. Keep me very close to you all my life then take me home to heaven to be with you.

Prayers of Repentance

Lord, as I read the Gospels and look at the love, truth and goodness of the Lord Jesus, help me to see how far I've fallen short of what you meant me to be. Let me stop comparing myself with other people and compare myself with you instead. Make me sorry for my life which is so unlike Jesus, and help me to be a better person.

✶✶✶

Lord, I want to tell you about the wrong things in my life. Thank you that as I confess them you have promised to forgive. Thank you too for forgiving those sins I have forgotten about. If I have wronged another person, help me to put it right with them as well as with you. If I have taken what is not mine, help me to give it back. If I have told a lie help me to say that it was not true. If I have quarrelled or hurt anyone, help me to say I am sorry.

Remove my sin, and I will be clean; wash me and I will be whiter than snow... Close your eyes to my sins and wipe out all my evil. Create a clean heart in me, and put a new and loyal spirit in me. (Psalm 51: 7-10)

Examine me, O God, and know my mind; test me and discover my thoughts. Find out if there is any evil way in me and guide me in the everlasting way. (Psalm 139:23-24)

Lord, I know that you loved the world and died to save sinners from their sin. So today I bring my sin to your cross. I want to confess it and turn away from it. I want to be forgiven. I believe that you love me. I take you now as my own Saviour, and I give myself to you to be yours for ever. For God so loved me that he gave his only son so that if I believe in him I may not die but will have eternal life. (John 3:16)

Search the Bible Answers

Search the Bible 1: Hannah prayed while moving her lips but no sound came out at all. She was praying for a baby. Jonah prayed in a whale.

Search the Bible 2: Eyes, ears and face.

Search the Bible 3: Broken bones; Terrors at night; arrow that flies by day (or any weapon), pestilence and plaugues (disease).

Search the Bible 4: Nehemiah was asked the question by the King — he gave what would have been a very quick prayer to God for help — before answering him. It must have been an instantaneous prayer or what some people call an arrow prayer. That is when you shoot a prayer up to God just like an arrow — quick and to the point. God answered Nehemiah's prayer as in the next sentence the King is arranging for Nehemiah to visit his home town — which is what Nehemiah had hoped for.

Search the Bible 5: Moses and Miriam gave thanks for God's salvation; David said sorry for his sins; Jesus prayed for the followers he was leaving behind and those, like us, who hadn't even been born yet.

Search the Bible 6: Daniel was in the habit of praying three times a day. When the other servants spotted him he was reported to the king and eventually thrown in the lion's den. Daniel had of course known about the King's decree and was well aware of what might happen — but prayer was so important to him, he couldn't stop it — no matter what.

Search the Bible 7: Joyful; Gentle and Thankful; do not be anxious. The key thing God tells us to do in these verses is pray: in everything present your requests to God — and then God will give us his peace which will guard our hearts and minds in Christ Jesus.

Search the Bible 8: In Mark 12:40 The Pharisees or Teachers of the Law made long prayers, pretending they were very holy but in actual fact they were destroying widows' houses — they would be punished for their sins. In Luke 18: 9-14 we see the Proud Pharisee who prayed to God as if God would be very pleased to hear from such an important man as him. Then we see the Tax Collector who prayed, 'God have mercy on me a sinner.' The Pharisee was proud. The Tax Collector was humble. If you exalt yourself you will be humbled and if you humble yourself God will exalt you.

Search the Bible 9: The prayer of the righteous is powerful and effective.

Search the Bible 10: All God's people or all the saints; those who mistreat you; pray for yourself that you do not fall into sin and temptation.

PATRICIA ST JOHN

Patricia St John was born in 1919 in England. In the early 1950's she went to Tangier, Morocco. She served in Morocco as a missionary nurse for 27 years. Patricia also travelled in Europe, North Africa, and the Middle East, as the settings of her novels reflect. In 1977 she returned to England, where she cared for elderly relatives and ministered from her home to youths, single parents, and the elderly. Her books, enjoyed by generations of readers, have been translated into numerous foreign languages.

THE SAFE PLACE

BY

PATRICIA ST JOHN

In the heat of a sleepy summer's afternoon the farm hand is dozing by the haystack when disaster strikes. A cigarette is carelessly discarded and very soon the whole haystack is on fire. By the end of the afternoon the whole barn has been destroyed and only the farmhouse is still standing. Most of the livestock have escaped to the fields but the little white hen and her chicks are missing.

Where is the little white hen and has she found a safe place for her chickens?

Read Patricia St John's heartwarming story of love and sacrifice, the perfect illustration of the Lord Jesus Christ's own love for his people when he died on the cross to save them.

ISBN 1-85792-779-6

TWICE FREED

PATRICIA ST. JOHN

TWICE FREED

BY

PATRICIA ST JOHN

Onesimus is a slave to the rich landlord Philemon and his son Archippus. But for Onesimus there is one glorious hour of freedom, every day, when the rest of the villa is asleep. It is then that he escapes to the hills and valley's surrounding the fields and vineyards of Philemon. Here he can be free - or at least pretend to be. And when he bumps into a mysterious young woman in the mountains he has no way of knowing how she will change his life forever. He helps the beautiful young, Eirene, and returns her to her rich family. But now what used to be a day dream never leaves Onesimus's mind. He must be free if he is ever to win the heart and hand of the merchant's young daughter. Find out how Onesimus copes with his longings and desire for freedom and discover how his acquaintance with Paul leads to freedom - twice over.

ISBN: 1-85792-4894

A Young Person's
GUIDE
To Knowing God

Patricia St John

A YOUNG PERSON'S GUIDE TO KNOWING GOD

BY

PATRICIA ST JOHN

God... Who is he? What does he do? How does a person get to know him? It would help if he told you a bit about himself - perhaps gave you a guidebook to help you along the way... Well, The Bible, is just that. Written by himself with the clever use of human beings as messengers, God's book is relevant, life changing and adventurous.

Patricia St John discovered this early on in her life and has written her own guide book to encourage and help young people to get into God's ultimate guide book - his Word. Based on the Apostles Creed this is an excellent devotional book for children and resource book for children's and young people's talks.

ISBN: 1-85792-5580

How To Handle Your Life...

and other helpful advice from God

Carine MacKenzie

HOW TO HANDLE YOUR LIFE

BY

CARINE MACKENZIE

There are all sorts of things about life that make it hard, difficult and down right confusing. Carine Mackenzie's book of short stories and puzzles is a great way of finding out about what God says about the whole thing. Get some good advice from the one who created life in the first place and made it to be good.

ISBN 1-85792-5203

How God Used A

THUNDERSTORM

And Other Devotional Stories

Joel R. Beeke & Diana Kleyn

Illustrated by Jeff Anderson

THE
BUILDING
ON THE
ROCK
SERIES

HOW GOD USED A THUNDERSTORM

BY

JOEL BEEKE

In this book of fascinating true life short stories you will discover other stories of how God has rescued and saved so many of his people. Find out how if it wasn't for a thunderstorm one woman would not have found out about the love of God for her. In this series there are four other books each with exciting and thrilling stories that tell you about how God does wonderful things in people's lives. Prayer points and Bible readings are included.

DANGER
ON THE HILL

CATHERINE MACKENZIE

Torchbearers

Danger On The Hill

by C. Mackenzie

"Run, run for your lives," a young boy screamed. "Run, everybody, run. The soldiers are here."

That day on the hill is the beginning of a new and terrifying life for the three Wilson children. Margaret, Agnes and Thomas are not afraid to stand up for what they believe in, but it means that they are forced to leave their home and their parents for a life of hiding on the hills.

If you were a covenanter in the 1600s you were the enemy of the King and the authorities. But all you really wanted to do was worship God in the way he told you to in the Bible. Margaret wants to give Jesus Christ the most important place in her life, and this conviction might cost her life. **There is danger on the hill for Margaret. There is danger everywhere - if you are a covenanter. The** Torchbearers series are true life stories from history where Christians have suffered and died for their faith in Christ.

ISBN 1 85792 7842

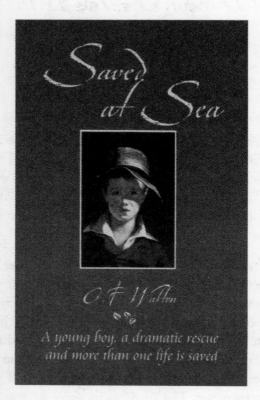

Saved at Sea

O. F. Walton

A young boy, a dramatic rescue
and more than one life is saved

Classic Fiction

Saved at Sea

by O. F. Walton

The waves are rising and the ship is on the rocks. Alick and his grandfather set out in their boat to save as many lives as they can... but this time they only come back with one. A little girl is thrown overboard moments before a huge wave sweeps the wreck away. Who is she? Where are her parents? What are they going to do?

As the storm disappears on the horizon, the little mystery girl touches the hearts of some very lonely people. Another stranger arrives on the island and Alick finds out that there is a rock that you can depend on in life, whatever the storms throw at you. Jesus Christ will always be there - an anchor, a fortress, stronger than a lighthouse on the rocks, stronger even than death!

ISBN: 1-85792-795-8